BEYOND THE VISIBLE
A True Story of Divine Encounters

Wauna Johnson

Copyright © 2008 by Wauna Johnson

Beyond The Visible
A True Story of Divine Encounters
by Wauna Johnson

Printed in the United States of America

ISBN 978-1-60647-359-7

All rights reserved solely by the author. The author guarantees all contents are original and do not infringe upon the legal rights of any other person or work. No part of this book may be reproduced in any form without the permission of the author. The views expressed in this book are not necessarily those of the publisher.

Unless otherwise indicated, Bible quotations are taken from The New King James Version of the Bible. Copyright © 1982 by Thomas Nelson Publishers.

www.xulonpress.com

Preface

What an incredibly awesome God we serve. I had to take the time to recall His wondrous works in my life. Through the trials and tests, He was always present. My desire for you, the reader, is to know God on a more intimate level. The miracles in the Bible and the ones we experience are just a foretaste of what is to come.

Read this book with an open mind. Pray about anything the Lord quickens to your spirit. And most of importantly, have faith in Jesus. Enjoy!

God bless!

Dedication

This book is dedicated to my children,
Elijah, Rachel and Isaiah,
"I love you dearly"

CONTENTS

Chapter 1 .... The Missing Link 11
Chapter 2 .... By His Wounds 23
Chapter 3 .... Ministering Spirits 35
Chapter 4 .... Festival of the Shelters 45
Chapter 5 .... Divine Protection 57
Chapter 6 .... The Other Realm 69
Chapter 7 .... Believing Without Seeing 75

1

The Missing Link

As a young girl growing up in the south suburbs of Chicago, I was no stranger to poverty, drugs and violence. My grandmother, bless her heart, practically raised all fifteen of my cousins and me in a four-bedroom, rundown house along with nine cats, two dogs and a songbird. Privacy was unheard of. We slept on couches or four to a bed and made paddles on the floor. In addition, there was only one working sink located down in the dark, junk-storage area called the basement. The wood beneath the flooring was weathered to the point that we could identify the bark on the panels. And food, well, it was as rare as dodo birds. "Granny, somebody ate the last bologna!" I remember pouting one day. She replied, "Well, you'll just have to eat a syrup sandwich." Yes, we redefined "sticky fingers." I lived in poverty my entire childhood. Worse, we never knew the true meaning of affection. Saying "I love you"

was like having an ape for a pet; it was unheard of and considered illegal.

Where were our parents? Well, they were either working all day and night, or simply missing in action. I never knew my biological father as a child and my mother, bless her heart, did the best she could with what she had. In this type of environment, children just find things to get into. We were exposed to sex in what we watched on TV in the downstairs bedroom when Granny went grocery shopping. Trying to find an escape, I spent most of my time sleeping and dreaming of a better life.

My grandmother was an advocate of going to church. When the Jehovah's Witnesses came by, she welcomed them in with open arms, but never allowed herself to be drawn away from the local church. The pastor would come by to pick her up, along with the kids who had no choice. After a while, I actually began to look forward to going. It was a small Lutheran church in the neighborhood. The pastor was the only positive male role model that we had since the death of our grandfather in 1979. Even though he was white and we were black, color was never an issue; he genuinely showed concern for our well being. I was comfortable sharing with him my dreams of pursuing an art degree. He helped me set goals and gave me constant encouragement. He believed in me more than I did. Actually, he encouraged all of us to pursue our dreams. Yet, as supportive as he was, deep down inside something was missing. I used to think that it was the absence of my biological father that had caused this void, but I was wrong.

During my high school years, I was rather withdrawn. The sting of rejection, not fitting in with the "in crowd," wounded me even more. You see, I was the skinny, knock-kneed girl who wasn't dressed in the latest fads and was often teased. All I had to lean on was my art talent. Creating art was the only time anyone paid attention to me. My high school art teacher thought my work was great and entered it into local contests and school galleries. She made me feel so special, because she believed in me.

My desire for acceptance was painfully obvious. I used to follow my oldest sister around like a shadow, wishing I had the popularity, beauty and social grace that she seemed to be born with. Then something amazing happened to me; I think they call it puberty.

Senior year was quite interesting. For once, guys were noticing me and I was noticing them. "Looking for Love in All the Wrong Places" was my theme song. I lost my virginity; or, should I say, I freely gave it away. Boyfriend after boyfriend, I became promiscuous, having tried almost every flavor of the rainbow. I was addicted to the brief "high" of feeling loved and desired by another that sex offered. Afterwards, the emptiness always resurfaced, along with hurt emotions and unhealthy attachments to my partner. Yet, that didn't stop me. I continued to expose myself, hoping that, I would meet Mr. Right someday.

Finally, the opportunity to do something worthwhile with my life presented itself. One of my close girlfriends had a sudden urge to join the military.

She boasted about how the recruiter painted this military utopia. "We get paid every two weeks, we get to travel and see the world and the men! We'll be surrounded by fine men all the time! On top of that, they'll even pay for your college education!" she exclaimed. Listening to her aroused my interest, until I discovered she was talking about the Marines. Their motto was "A Few Good Men," not women. As I sat there listening to the recruiter, I gazed around the office and noticed a poster with a female Marine hanging on the wall. She was immaculately dressed in uniform, yet still feminine. I stared at her and thought, "this may just work." And so I came to join the Marines.

My mother was first to hear the news. She was really excited for me, as was Granny. For the first time ever, I got the opportunity to leave the poverty-stricken suburb and venture out into the world. The first stop was boot camp in South Carolina. My stomach fluttered with anticipation. When we finally arrived, a female Marine boarded the bus and instructed us to keep quiet and follow the yellow footsteps on the pavement. Okay, we're in OZ, that's what took so long. Anyway, after us "new recruits" settled into our open bay quarters, we met the drill instructors.

One by one, they were introduced to us, as we sat staring in amazement on the bay floor. If Hulk Hogan had sisters, surely these were them. Their legs were bigger than my whole body, and their faces displayed the essence of intimidation. I just knew we were in for the trial of our lives. Twelve more weeks of hell lay ahead. Rushing here and there, exercising in ant pits, marching in the scorching sun, carrying around rifles and war gear, kissing up to She-Ra's, the constant screaming and yelling, playing G I Jane in the jungle—this was not what I expected. Why did I let my friend talk me into this? I couldn't wait for it to end. Over and over, I tried to repeat in my mind what the recruiter advised when he said, "It's mind over matter; when you pass boot camp, you'll be a Marine."

Finally, the end of the torment arrived, with the exception of one final lesson to complete—the swimming qualification. There were four of us who still needed to pass. We didn't have any swimming pools in my neighborhood, so I never learned how to swim. Not only that, they made us swim with heavy war gear strapped to our bodies. My pack was so weighty, I sank every time I got in the water. The DI's were aggravated with us "swim flunks" and I didn't know if I was going to graduate.

On the last day to qualify, the most inscrutable thing happened. I jumped in the water, as usual, and anchored to the bottom. In the previous attempts, I would sink almost immediately. But it didn't happen this time. Instead, I felt a big thrust from beneath the water and my cargo pants had somehow attached to my rifle, propelling me backwards. As a result, my pack became a floating device. No one else was in the water with me; I was the last needing to qualify. I remembered drifting across the water while glancing into the clear blue sky. Time passed quickly and, the next thing I knew, I had made it to the finish line and passed. Puzzled and overjoyed by what had taken place, I left that experience pondering if something outside of the norm had occurred, too illogical for explanation. For once, I thought about the existence of God.

A week later, I graduated and became a Marine. The achievement was overwhelming; I had never fathomed I would accomplish anything of that nature. My family was so proud of me. Everyone was excited to hear about the experience. The respect and love shown at that moment was unforgettable; yet, as exciting and thrilling as this achievement was, something was still missing in my life. The void wasn't filled. But I had to move on. And so, the journey began, onto the real thing, Marine Corp life.

My first tour of duty was in Okinawa, Japan. I had never heard of this island or even known of its existence. Just the thought of leaving the country was a little intimidating, let alone leaving to some remote island in the middle of the ocean. Yet, after that boot camp experience, nothing was too shocking anymore. The flight was more than twenty-two hours long. You could feel the humidity of the climate from the airplane; it felt like 110 degrees or more. When we departed the plane, I thought I was going to pass out or suffocate from the heat. "Ah, you'll get use to it," is what I heard when the pickup crew arrived.

I soon discovered that there weren't a lot of female Marines. We were like a rare commodity; sought after and, I might add, greatly desired. Of course, this was exactly what I did not need. As soon as I got the opportunity to explore and venture out, I seized it. My initial intention to carry a demure disposition was short lived. The independence and admiration received boosted my ego. Trying to be discreet, I hid my lust under the disguise of relationships with boyfriends, until one day, when I received the most inconceivable and shocking news: I was pregnant.

My youth abruptly ended. More devastating, the father didn't want anything to do with his unborn child. He urged me to get an abortion, but something deep down inside wouldn't allow me to do it. It just felt wrong. For weeks I was discombobulated. What in the world was I supposed to do with a baby? How was I going to take care of it? I just started my career as a Marine and, at nineteen, I barely knew how to take care of myself. To top it all off, I was thousands of miles away from home in a foreign country.

No longer the cream of the crop, I was treated like the black sheep in the family. My friends scattered, leaving me to deal with this issue alone. No one seemed to care anymore. I was forced to continue the rigid exercise routine despite my fragile condition. They told me "you were not issued a baby when you got that rifle." During the first trimester, I became extremely ill with nausea. Everything I ate, I threw up. I was hospitalized numerous times for dehydration. No one understood the condition; I just had to suffer through it. At this point, I really didn't know what would become of life. My future looked so bleak.

When my overseas tour ended, they assigned me to my new duty station in Cherry Point, North Carolina—within a month of delivery. My mother came down for the birth and to help during the recovery. After witnessing the delivery, her knees became so weak she could hardly walk; yet, elated at the sight her grandchild, we both cried in felicity. He looked just liked me. I soon forgot the painful experience of childbirth. However, even this amazing event failed to answer the missing link dilemma.

I had no clue how to be a mother. The financial responsibility of raising a child was quite challenging. Somehow, I made it through without doing too much damage to either of us. My private life became centered on my child. Dating was not on the agenda.

We resided in Cherry Point for about three years before my next assignment. At that point, I had the option of getting out or re-enlisting. Well, the fact that I was a single parent lacking work experience, the decision was apparent. So I opted for another four year term and went back to the island of Okinawa. This time, I was determined to keep myself focused. My plans were simple—raise my son, save money, and continue college.

My son, at two and a half, was just learning to talk, run and get into things. On my to-do list was to find us a church. I learned from the Lutheran faith that Sunday is the Lord's Day and church attendance was not optional. Looking through the local military paper, I noticed an ad for a Baptist church. It was the only American church listed, so I made plans to attend. I had never been to a Baptist church before. The church was located off base, in the community of Okinawa. In contrast to the U.S., there were no sidewalks, very few street signs, extremely narrow roads, and the traffic was wreck prone. In addition, they have a "three-second rule" that permits passage through a red light after three seconds. On top of all that, they drove on the opposite side of the road.

Finally we arrived. As we entered the church, quite a few things were different traditionally from what I was accustomed to. First, everybody was African American; nothing wrong with that, so am I. Second, they didn't have a program. How was I supposed to know the order of service or what to sing? To my surprise, the words to the songs were displayed on overhead projectors and people were lifting their hands and shouting "Halleluiah!" I thought church was the only other place besides the library where silence was the Golden Rule. Furthermore, almost everyone was dressed formally. I felt out of place wearing my sandals, shirt and shorts.

As I listened to the preacher, I got this strange impression that he was talking about me. Almost everything he said made me squirm on the bench. I began to look around the sanctuary to see if I knew anyone. I was certain that someone had gossiped about me and told the preacher, but I didn't know anyone there. Towards the end of the service, another preacher came forward and began to beckon to the congregation for all wanting to accept Jesus as their Lord and Savior to come forward. Once again, I had never heard this terminology before. It was peculiar.

At the Lutheran church, we were taught to honor and respect the house of God through humble reverence and silence. The emphasis was more on

Christ the Divine rather than Christ the Person. Your church attendance and confession of belief established your salvation. However, this was not the underlying doctrine of the Baptist church. As I sat there listening, the palms of my hands began to sweat and my stomach fluttered. The awkwardness of the moment prevented me from stepping forward. On the way home, all I could think about was that experience. Eager to revisit, I was determined to find an explanation. The following week, the tugging reoccurred, but this time I was compelled from within to take those steps towards the front.

At the altar, the deacon guided me into a prayer of repentance and acceptance of Jesus as God's Son, who died on the cross for my sins, rose from the grave and is seated in Heaven at the right hand of God the Father. From that moment on, my life was not the same. Later that day, I noticed a sudden change in my son's behavior from hyperactive to serene. Something had definitely happened.

Prayer, direct communication with God, was emphasized at this church. The ability to have my very own personal relationship with Jesus, the One whom I had read about every week at Sunday school, was truly remarkable. Not only that, He knows all about me. For once, I found a stable comfort zone. The more I came back to church, the better I began to feel. I was intrigued by the expounding of the scriptures; like a starved lion, I was hungry for more. They taught through prayer that we can talk to God and He actually listens. But it doesn't end there, He answers! It was truly amazing! I could talk to Jesus about anything, anywhere, and at anytime. This was what my heart yearned for, a genuine relationship with someone who wouldn't judge or leave me; someone who understood and had the answers to life. Besides that, He sacrificed His life for me, as the scripture states in John 3:16, "For God so loved the world that He gave His only begotten Son, and whosoever believes in Him, shall not perish, but have everlasting life." I was headed straight to hell with gasoline pants on and didn't even realize it. But thank God for Jesus, who willfully traded places with me. From that moment on, I was totally persuaded and committed to follow Jesus.

The pastor began to preach about the Holy Spirit and how He is the agent behind salvation. He went on to say that the Holy Spirit is God's Spirit, one of the three in the trinity—Father, Son and Holy Ghost. Boy, I really had a lot to learn. Up until then, I thought that church attendance was a way to pay my "spiritual dues" to a God that seemed unapproachable. At this church, they emphasized the importance of baptism. I remembered getting baptized at the Lutheran church; however, I was unaware of its biblical significance then, so I decided to get baptized again.

On the day of my baptism, the excitement I felt was intense. What was going to happen? Would I feel the Holy Spirit or a tangible presence of God? Well, to my surprise, I went down in the water and came out wet. If something was supposed to happen, I think I missed it. On the other hand, I now had a better understanding of baptism. In the Christian faith, baptism links the baptized person's identity to Christ in His death, burial and resurrection.

My bible became my best friend. I read it every day, first thing in morning, right before breakfast. I believed everything written in it, all the stories and promises from the Red Sea parting to Jesus casting out devils. Of course, I had to tell my family about this. At first, I was hesitant to share the news, being wary of ridicule. Yet, something inside of me tugged on my heart. One day, I called my mother and told her I was saved and that I had given my life to Christ. Her response went something like, "Oh, that's nice baby. So when are you coming home?" I knew that she had to experience what I did in order to understand. From then on, I started praying for my family to receive Christ into their lives. I knew He wanted them saved too.

I learned that the people that God placed in my life, my family, pastors, teachers and the events up to that point were not coincidental. Thankfully, God was behind it all. Even when I didn't know Him, He knew me. Nothing in my life would be wasted. Finally, I found the missing link; it was Jesus.

"I knew you before you were formed in your mother's womb."
Jeremiah 1:5

2

By His Wounds

Life was good at church, home, and work. One day, a young Marine stopped by the office, and my sergeant got this bright idea to play cupid. He told me that the young man was really a nice guy; in fact, he faithfully attended church, too. Still, my mind was made up—no men. Unfortunately, it wasn't long until my intentions changed. Suddenly, I found myself thinking about him. The next the thing I knew, we were dating.

Soon, our pastors discovered we were dating. I must admit, things were moving rather rapidly. I remember praying about him, but I didn't wait to get an answer. Besides, I was unsure on how to determine the Lord's will; I had only been saved for a month. Nevertheless, I convinced myself that he was the one. We told our pastors we were serious about each other. "Y'all really need to go ahead and do the right thing, GET MARRIED!" they so tenderly exclaimed. Informal pre-marital counseling at its best. With only a few months in the relationship, I accepted his proposal.

After informing my mother of our marriage plans, she replied, "Call me back in about a month." My senior authority in the chain of command just laughed at us. They made me wonder if this was a good decision. Anyway, we proceeded with the plans. Off we went to the Japanese American Consultant. They married us and sent us away with a license in Kanji (Japanese writing) without any pre-nuptial agreement. We decided to postpone the formal celebration until we returned to the U.S. For the next three years, we grew to know each other and he bonded well with my son.

After a year into the marriage, I was given a temporary assignment to Thailand. Before entering the country, we were debriefed on the climate and culture of the natives. The people in this country were very different from the Okinawans; not only in physical appearance, but in tradition. More than 80 percent of the population, including the animals, were infected with some sort of disease. They worshiped statues of different shapes and sizes. For safety reasons, we were forewarned not to engage in any sexual relations with the natives. Alarmed by the debriefing, I wanted out of this assignment, but they refused my request.

When we entered the country, I noticed that the traffic there was worse than in Japan. There were no speed limits or traffic lights. We bunked in humid concrete barrack houses. The toilets didn't flush, so we made portable outhouses out of large trash bags covered with wooden lids. One day, I saw the natives bathing and brushing their teeth with muddy rain water that collected in the bottom of concrete barrels. However, this wasn't the worst thing. Along the squalid streets and alleys lay incapacitated men, women and children. Some of them were plagued with terrible skin diseases and amputations, and all were extremely impoverished. My heart filled with pity. I longed to help all of them, but I was limited by resources and time; prayer was my only recourse. I knew the Lord wanted to help them.

Many of the women were deceptively beautiful, while a majority of the men were transvestites; they made their livelihoods as prostitutes. Sadly, the husbands of the women allowed them to partake in this trade. They became victims to their circumstances. Upon departure, some of the soldiers didn't heed the warning in the lecture and were infected with a multitude of STD's, even HIV. One Marine entered the country with a minor incision on his arm. His occupation forced him to work in the contaminated waters. After a month, the incision became infected and spread across his arm. The doctors discovered that cancer had set in on his arm and amputation was the only remedy.

It appeared to be an atmosphere inundated with evil. Onc of my fellow church members asked me if I had trouble praying. As of matter of fact, I did. My concentration was broken, making it difficult to pray. It was as though an antagonistic force hindered it. But I prayed anyway. They shortened the assignment and

I returned home safely, thanks to be to God. Little did I know, my own healing crisis was awaiting me in the near future.

A year after this short assignment, my husband and I discovered we were pregnant. Unfortunately, the pregnancy was not blissful. Once again, the agonizing symptoms resurfaced—nausea, vomiting and dehydration. This time, it was much worse. I spent the entire pregnancy in and out of the hospital. The medication I received through the IV's burned my veins, causing intense pain and bruising. When they did send me home, I slept with a basin by the bed due to the frequent vomiting. To make matters worse, I had to carry around this disgusting spit cup. People thought I was chewing tobacco. It gets better. Because of the frequent heaving, I tore the lining around my stomach, which caused blood to appear in my vomit. It was a horrible experience. The elders of the church came by to pray for me, but I didn't seem to get better. Our pastor told me to blame Eve. "What does Eve have to do with my suffering?" I wondered. According to the story in Genesis, God told Eve she would have pain in childbirth, He didn't say anything about sickness. I guess the pastor was trying to console us in our misery.

The doctors instructed me to stay hydrated. They diagnosed me with a rare disease called Hyperemesis: a potentially life-threatening pregnancy disease marked by rapid weight loss, malnutrition, and dehydration due to unrelenting nausea and/or vomiting with potentially adverse consequences for the newborn. I had never felt so helpless in my life, not to mention, I was terribly concern for my baby. Physically, I looked like a vampire had sucked the life out of me. My skin was grossly pale and my arms were like wire hangers. I wondered what was going through my husband's mind. He was calm and supportive, but bewildered, I'm sure. This was a major challenge for us, especially being newlyweds. Unfortunately, I remained in that condition until her birth. I even threw up during the delivery.

Finally, she was born, healthy and with all ten fingers and toes. Thankfully, the agony had ended. However, I questioned God about the experience. I didn't understand why I was not healed before the delivery. I remember hearing the stories of how Jesus, Paul, Peter, and others had laid hands on people and healed them. I thought that maybe healing was for certain people, or perhaps I didn't deserve it. The mystery would soon be unraveled.

We had two years remaining on our overseas tour. My husband's enlistment had ended early and he sought employment as a civilian. The last year on the island opened my eyes to the realization that there was another war in progress.

My husband's new boss was a senior female Marine who just happened to be a minister, at least that's what she told everybody. She called our house at unusual hours, insisting that my husband work on his off time. Almost every conversation was doused in her spirituality. Then she started asking too many questions, prying into our personal business. Immediately, I prayed for my husband to get another job, but he was stuck there. Besides, we needed to save money for the transition back to the states.

After a while, I became annoyed and reprimanded her for her behavior—big mistake; it only made matters worse. So I consulted our pastor for guidance. "Jezebel, she's got a Jezebel spirit. You need to read second Kings and pray," he advised. A Jezebel Spirit! What in the world was that? I read the story in the bible and discovered she was an evil queen who ruled over God's people and her husband, King Ahab. She killed the Lord's prophets and influenced the people to worship foreign gods and partake in immoral practices. The question now was how to apply this knowledge to our situation.

One day, while at my hair stylist's house, I told her about it. She asked me if I had the gift of the Holy Spirit, speaking in tongues. "Isn't that for pastors and ministers only?" I asked. Her eyes bulged off her face. "Of course not! You can receive the gift right now! Do you want to pray?" I agreed and immediately she grasped my hands and started speaking in a strange language, "Econdallalala-bowshy!" She told me to open up my mouth and speak. All the while I felt fiery jolts shoot down from her hands into mine. As I opened my mouth, a knot fixed itself in my throat. Suddenly, something sprung from my vocals, I couldn't make it out. Amazed and overwhelmed by what happened, I went home and sat down on the bed in awe, reading the scriptures on tongues.

At bible study, the pastor taught on the subject. He said the gift of the tongues comes by faith, just like salvation. He stressed how, when we speak in tongues, the devil cannot understand what we are saying. It is direct communication with God that builds up our most holy faith. Not only that, praying in tongues translates the perfect will of God to heaven. I practiced speaking until it became fluent and a part of my prayer life. Upon departure, the boss lady spoke very positively about my husband. The phone calls ceased and the tensions between us resolved. This experience opened my eyes. The other war is a spiritual one, and I needed to be prepared.

As we tried to decide where to migrate, Chicago or Houston, my husband sold me on Houston. We stayed with his parents until we got settled. On the to-do list, we needed to find a church, and I stressed this point. In response, he replied, "That church stuff was back in Japan, we're in the states now." The enemy used this doorway to wreak havoc on our marriage.

Within six months we exhausted the resources we had saved and stayed with his parents longer than anticipated. My husband secured a job before we left Japan and I got into real estate. His income wasn't quite enough to support a family of three and I wasn't having any success in the home business. We were reduced to borrowing money from his parents. To make matters worse, he was no longer interested in the church. As a result, our marriage began to fail.

My husband was raised with a totally different set of values than mine. In his family, loyalty was priority over anything or anyone, even God. In my family, independence from family was priority— every man or woman for themselves. Truthfully, we both came from dysfunctional families that only

Jesus could array. Yet, after becoming a member of God's family, I was taught that commitment to our families should never compromise the biblical foundation of our faith. Unfortunately, he was not amiable. As a byproduct, numerous disputes, misunderstandings and divided loyalties between his family and I surfaced. As much as I desired, trying to adapt was nearly impossible. One day he told me, "We are all one big family and I will always be loyal to my family." We desperately needed family counseling from a spiritual source.

Amid this marital breakdown, I discovered I was pregnant. Once again, those terrible symptoms resurfaced—nausea, vomiting, and dehydration, in and out of the hospital. The medication they prescribed for the nausea made me extremely lethargic. Unable to care for myself and family, I was forced to quit my job. Why was all of this happening to me? What did I do to deserve this? Besides, I was totally committed to my walk with God, attended church faithfully, read my bible every day, remained loyal to husband, loved my children—I just couldn't understand it. After about five months of torture, I began to internalize my life and my faith in God. Why is God allowing me to suffer like this? Surely, he cares about what I'm going through.

As I was lying on the couch watching Christian television, they showed Jesus ascending into the sky saying, "Lo, I am with you even until the end of the world." That image remained embedded in mind. Then, suddenly, a small voice began to quote the scriptures in my ear. I heard "all things work together for good to those who loved God and are called." It went on to say, "By His stripes, you are healed." The voice said, "Get up, get up! You are healed!" Those words rang louder and louder in my ears until I lifted myself off the couch. It was the Lord. I began to repeat those scriptures aloud and envisioned myself well.

Over the next couple of weeks, my health was restored. The nausea ceased and my appetite returned, along with renewed energy. My son was born healthy and I had the strength to deliver him naturally. Praise the Lord! He healed me. He miraculously healed me!

A miracle is defined as an occurrence that is unusual and goes beyond the laws of nature.

Now, what was the difference between this pregnancy and the last? It was faith. I had to believe that I was healed in order to receive it. God's power to heal is very real. I had heard these scriptures numerous times at church and through reading, but never took the time to apply them to my life. Since this experience, they have taken on a new meaning. Faith is a very important part of receiving answers to prayers.

Furthermore, my understanding of sickness and healing had changed. I used to think that suffering was a direct result of sin, like the victims in Thailand. After reading Job, I realized this thinking was not biblical, but legalistic. Satan attacked Job, yet God turned it around to bless Job. None of my "good deeds" or conduct produced the healing—it was faith in Jesus that healed me. The Lord always wanted me healed during my pregnancies. Boy, I still have so much to learn about this Christian life.

A year later, my mother called to inform me that she had contacted my father. I wasn't expecting this surprise. After twenty-six years of mystery, for the first time ever, I got to speak with him. I held back the tears until I hung up. That same day, I spoke to his mother who sent information about our family background and heritage. The pieces of my lost identity fell into place. My husband agreed to take a trip to Chicago to meet my lost family; maybe he hoped this visit would help me understand his perspective.

At twenty-six years of age, I met my biological father. My youngest son resembled him. We hugged and cried and hugged and cried. On my father's side, there were black people, white people, Indians and others—a melting pot of races. My entire life, I grew up thinking I was half a person with a muffled identity because I had no father. When I saw him, all of the unanswered questions vanished. Now, this enigma is solved and I had to thank the Lord for healing this emotional wound that had lain dormant for so many years.

When we returned home, we were invited to a baby dedication at a non-denominational church. It was a relatively small congregation, no more than about thirty active members. The pastor had this special gift of prophecy, where he was given insight into spiritual things. His prophetic insight was so precise, it was almost scary. I never saw this gift operating in a person, so I was curious to study the topic. In 1 Corinthians 12, the entire chapter is dedicated to identifying and explaining the spiritual gifts that the Holy Spirit bestows on individuals for the work of God.

We decided to join this church. Every week we attended, along with my in-laws. During the first service, the Lord exposed the nature of our marital crisis and offered words of encouragement. My heart was overjoyed. The church became a buffer zone. I convinced my husband that we should have this pastor counsel us and he agreed. The pastor read the scripture in Genesis 24, which states that a man leaves his mother and father and is joined to his wife, and the two of them become one flesh. The separation is not exclusively spatial; rather, the husband's priorities change from parents to wife and children. As simple as it sounded, it was difficult for him to grasp as he stated, "If I have to choose between my wife and my mother, I choose my mother—I can always get another wife."

One Sunday during worship service, I felt the presence of God overtake me. My destitute spirit cried out to God and he heard. As I lifted up my hands, the words from Ezekiel 47 echoed from the pulpit to my spirit. The healing waters that slowly emerged Ezekiel at increasing increments were now encompassing me. I drifted to the ground, drenched in the presence of God. In this state of bliss, tears trickled from my eyes as I lay there. Peace had marked my spirit. When I arose, I walked over to my in-laws and hugged them, I felt such compassion and love for them. They stared in amazement and asked if I was all right. Oh how I hoped this spiritual high would never end.

"And by His stripes we are healed."
Isaiah 53:5

3

Ministering Spirits

I tried everything in my power to keep the marriage intact. Unfortunately, his fastidious attitude coupled with his actions of indignity, adultery, and threats gradually led to the inevitable. Secretly, he made plans to divorce and keep the children. However, I could not fathom leaving my children. I stayed on my face in prayer. Contemplating whether or not to initiate the divorce, the Lord answered in the most astonishing manner. As I began to read the bible, it appeared to be reading me. The scripture from Malachi 2:16 was illuminated, where it stated, "For the Lord God of Israel says that He hates divorce, for it covers one's garment with violence." In addition, 1 Corinthians 7 says that if the unbeliever departs, let him depart.

From God's perspective, divorce is not a case of a hardened heart towards the other mate, but rather towards God, who admonishes us to walk in love. The bible says 1 Corinthians 13 that love is longsuffering, kind, doesn't envy or behave rudely, is not proud, thinks no evil, bears all things, and hopes all things. At the moment I wanted to divorce, love was not on the agenda, but rather grudges and anger. Only Jesus could help me walk in this kind of love and heal my brokenness. Not my will, His will be done.

The events that took place in the next few days would forever change my life. An overwhelming peace came over me. All the worries, concerns and fears came to an abrupt halt. The Lord began to communicate with me through my thoughts—a dialogue in my mind. His voice was clear as He began to give me instructions. He told me to transcribe the conversation. He informed me that He had chosen me to speak for Him and to say only what He tells me. His messages would be for His people. In addition, he assured me of His presence and help, forewarning that I would face persecution and insults.

This communication went on for about three days. Everything He said, I wrote down. Strangely, I was fully aware of my surroundings, functioning as though nothing was going on, but my mind was in a very elevated state, like a trance. During this period, my appetite ceased and I was fasting. At the end of the third day, I felt the trance ending. As my own thoughts slowly returned, the tranquility wore off. My mind was now again preoccupied with the marriage dilemma. However, after this divine encounter with the Lord, His voice was more distinct.

A trance is the displacing of the individual's ordinary state of mind with an elevated, God-given state for the purpose of instructing him. This is in line with the prophetic promise of dreams and visions given by the Holy Spirit to advance God's redemptive purposes.

The Lord granted me permission to leave with my children, without initiating divorce. Unaware of our next destination, we prudently exited. From that moment on, the Bible became like a road map, literally illustrating the scripture in Psalms 119:105, "Your word is a lamp to my feet and a light to my path." We received divine guidance that led us through the unknown journey. The Lord instructed us to contact my former childcare provider. We stayed with her for about two weeks. During this time, my husband began harassing my sister to learn our whereabouts. She prayed for us and served as a peaceful liaison amid this crisis. My prayer also was for healing and a peaceful resolution.

While at our friend's house, I continued to attend class at the university where I had recently enrolled—hoping I would finish the semester without interruption. On my way to class, I stopped at a gas station. There was a young man standing next to the entrance. He was a young, Italian-looking man with tattoos covering both of his arms. As I approached, he asked me for a ride. "Can I see your ID?" I hesitantly requested. After showing me his card, I asked him to wait while I pumped my gas. Out of the sky flashed a roaring thunder. The vibration caused both us to jump. Rain began to fall as I motioned him to come.

Praying that the Lord would keep me safe, I asked him where he was going. As it turned out, he was headed in the same direction as my school. He told me that he was selling subscriptions to magazines and his ride had left him stranded. The radio was on KSBJ Christian music. He recognized the artist singing and said that he enjoyed their music. We began talking about the church and Jesus. Then, he asked me a startling question. "Why did you hesitate to give me a ride?" he inquired. "Well, there's lots of strange people in the city and, being a female, I needed to be careful." He looked kind of puzzled by my response. We switched the subject back to church; all the while he was directing me towards his home. He lived in a town with a reputation for being prejudice against other races. I had never been there before. Unbeknownst to me, I would soon return.

About a week later, the Lord told me that my husband was coming and we needed to leave. As I prayed for help and guidance, the Lord answered. He asked me if I remembered the young man that I gave a ride. I said yes. He told me that the man was an angel. Now, this totally blew my mind. What kind of angel would have tattoos? The Lord took me to the scriptures in Hebrews 13:2 "Do not forget to entertain strangers, for by doing so some have unwittingly entertained angels." Furthermore, we are not to judge people by appearance. The Lord wanted me to recall where the angel took me. He told me to head in that direction, help was waiting. We bid our farewell to our friend and thanked her being a tremendous blessing to us.

The superiority of Christ is evident in His enthronement, while the angels are but ministers who serve both Christ and the saints.

As we entered the town, we headed towards the house where the man lived. To our amazement, the house was not there. What next? Well, I noticed a Holiday Inn at the entrance of the town, so we went there. The Lord confirmed in my spirit this was the place. The only problem was that I had exhausted all of our funds and could not afford an eighty-dollar-a-night room. But if the Lord said this was the place, then it must be. We began to talk to the clerk about our situation. He had been working there for some time and was sympathetic. As I was talking to him, a man approached the counter that he recognized. When the man left, the clerk informed me that he had just purchased a room and only spent thirty minutes using it. He let us stay in the room for the night. On top of that, he gave us twelve dollars for dinner. My heart was so overjoyed. I was convinced that the Lord was watching over our steps.

The next day, we ate a continental breakfast for free. At noon, we checked out and I didn't know where to go. The Lord wanted us to stay there another night. Well, I went back to the front desk. This time, there was a different clerk working. I told her our situation, but she could not help. As we walked out, an elderly man approached us. I felt the Lord wanted me to say something to him, but I didn't know what, so I prayed. When he left the front desk, I asked him if he could help us. He told me to go to the front desk and wait. He graciously paid for our room and gave us twenty dollars. Praise the Lord, another miracle!

That night, as I was reading, the Lord told me we had to move on. The next morning, Jesus gave very specific instructions. He instructed me to watch for these specific signs: A man in a hiding place, two horses—one reddish brown and the other ivory, some mulberry trees, the sun, and four winds in the sky. These five descriptions were found in the books of Isaiah and Zechariah. I told my children what the Lord said and asked them to help me find these signs. Early the next day, we ventured out, examining billboards, street markings, buildings—anything that resembled the signs.

The Holy Scriptures are called the revealed Word of God.

The sun beamed on these particular signs, which led to a new development of custom-built homes. "Halleluiah!" I was overly jubilant! I thought the Lord was going to miraculously provide us with a new house! Hovering over the subdivision, the children noticed four oblong cloud streaks arranged in a parallel manner. 'Look mama, in the sky!" That must be the sign of the four winds. As we entered, there were four sales offices. I didn't know which one to enter. When we entered the first home, a woman warmly welcomed us. She let us tour the house and gave us some information on the community and we left. As we drove away, the kids noticed the gated community across the driveway that was surrounded with thick trees (the sign for the mulberry trees). The guard granted us permission to look at more model homes in the community. We drove through at 3 miles per hour, trying find the other signs. My son noticed how the sun suddenly peaked through the clouds as if it were signaling to us. It stationed itself over a house, one of the model homes. I told the children this must be the place.

With bible in hand, we entered. The salesman was tucked under his desk in the garage office. After our greeting, he replied, "If you are interested in the home, we'll sell you the furniture too. All I have to do is pack up my little space." This was the sign for the man in a hiding place. He let us tour this beautifully decorated five-bedroom two-story home with an inside balcony. As we ventured up the stairs, I noticed a pastel portrait hanging at eye level. It featured two elegantly drawn horses, one was ivory and the other reddish brown—the last sign of confirmation. All I could do was stare. How awesome is our God!

Through divine guidance, the Lord led us here. "Is this salesman going to just give us the house?" Well, I thought I'd better be candid and tell him our story. To my disappointment, he wasn't very sympathetic. Perplexed by the experience, I went in prayer. By this time, the children were hungry. In the parking lot of a grocery store, I noticed a young lady approaching us and sensed she could help. As it turned out, she was a pastor's daughter. Their church was having a dinner and she invited us out. After meeting and speaking with the pastor, he advised me to return to my husband or get assistance from the local authorities. He was, however, gracious enough to pay for our room that night.

In the morning, the Lord said we were not to return to the hotel. So, I decided to return to the model home. Perhaps I missed something. When we got there, the man was gone and an elderly lady, his hostess, greeted us. I went into the bedroom and sat on the window sill and prayed. It was getting late and I informed the hostess we would return. Intentionally, I left my bible on the bed. When we returned, the hostess was holding my bible in her hand. "Are you guys okay?" she gently asked. I couldn't hold it in anymore and told her our story and how God had led us here. She just smiled and said, "I knew something was up." She referred us to some of the local ministries in the area, but they were all closed.

After driving around aimlessly, we headed back to the hotel and parked in the lot. To our surprise, the elderly lady and her husband were waiting on us. "I have been looking all over for you guys! Are you hungry?" She took us to Luby's and invited us to stay at her house. "I just couldn't get you all off of my mind," she repeatedly stated. It was Thanksgiving weekend and they wanted us to join them. We stayed with them for a few days. They were a pleasantly peaceful elderly couple, so considerate to open up their homes to complete strangers. They even bought a birthday cake for my son.

Unfortunately, we all agreed I couldn't stay there. I didn't want them to feel alarmed by the threat of my husband. They encouraged me to call the domestic abuse hotline and let them help us find a place. This didn't sound spiritual at all. I was frustrated and frightened. Why would the Lord send us to a shelter after showing us this gorgeous house? I didn't want my children to live in an unhealthy environment amongst a bunch of strangers who could be potentially dangerous. There must be another solution. But no, this was God's will.

"For He shall give His angels charge over you, to keep you in all your ways."
Psalm 91:11

4

Festival of the Shelters

The counselor from the domestic violence hotline gave us a referral list of shelters. Nanna, the elderly lady, located the closest one and prompted me to call them. They instructed us to drive to a police station and, from there, they would escort us to the facility. Anticipation and concern filled me. The children, on the other hand, acted as if we were going to a party. We pulled up to an old gated house surrounded by huge bushes. A video monitor mounted on a black steel gate at the entrance granted us permission to enter. There were about four other families, women and children, in this shelter.

We slept in a congested room with old wooden bunk beds and torn up closets. The cold concrete floors and scarce linens made it difficult to get comfortable. The first night, I hardly slept. A few days later, I discovered a ringworm rash on my arm. Without health insurance, I could only pray for a miracle. Within a couple of days, the ringworm had dried up and disappeared—thank you Jesus.

Our roommate was a young Hispanic girl, no older than twenty. She had no children of her own. Her boyfriend had beaten her severely and family disowned her. My heart went out to her. I told her about Jesus and how much he loved her. I asked her if she wanted to pray. Tears rolled down her face as she accepted Jesus as her Savior. Perhaps the Lord had led us there just for her. All of the women there were suffering from either physical or emotional abuse trauma. I knew that Jesus wanted to help them, just like He was helping us. One of the ladies suggested that we start a bible study. It was a great idea, but, unfortunately, our stay there was relatively short, only a month. They referred us to another shelter that was eighty miles up the highway. Little did we know, the Lord had more surprises in store.

The intake counselor met us at the Kroger's down the street from the shelter. They try to be as safe as possible with domestic-violence victims. Like the other shelter, this was a house located in an older neighborhood. The security wasn't as rigid. Inside, it was much more pleasant than the previous shelter. The flooring was a nice finished tile and each room had clean, durable beds. They even had a playroom for the children with a TV. It was a relaxing atmosphere, for a while. There were at least twelve or more other ladies; some had children, some didn't, but all were hurting. Once we got settled in, we made goals. I wanted to meet the ladies so I put an encouraging note on everyone's door about God's love for them.

Beyond The Visible

Some responded and the Lord gave us opportunities to pray and share our story.

The shelter staff conducted weekly counseling sessions. At one session, we played a social development card game. The cards contained questions relating to personality and social interests. One young girl, who was relatively new, chose a card about religion. She announced her religious affiliation of Wiccan and that her mother cast a protection spell over her before she came. She wore rings embossed with moons and cultic objects. Her nostrils and ears were completely punctured with jewelry. "A witch!" the ladies began to shriek. This was the last thing they needed. No one wanted this young lady near them. However, I felt compassion for her because she didn't appear harmful, just confused.

One day, a resident caught the young girl engaged in a private ceremony outside in the courtyard. Dancing and then kneeling before a rock, she was heard chanting strange noises and moaning. Reports of terrible bloody nightmares were shared among the residents. They all attributed it to the new housemate. As it turned out, these incidents drove the ladies to prayer and they wanted to start a bible study. We planned it after breakfast the next morning. They wanted me to do a lesson. I never formally taught a bible lesson, but I knew Jesus could use whatever I had. Everyone attended, included the young witch girl.

After the bible study, I asked if anyone wanted to pray to accept Christ into their hearts. To our surprise, the young lady raised her hand. She never heard the gospel of Jesus Christ, all she ever knew was Wicca. I explained to her that Jesus died on the cross for our sins so that we could live, according to John 3:16. Not only that, He defeated the forces of darkness so that we could live in victory. I told her how much the Lord loved her and desired to have an intimate relationship with her. We prayed a salvation prayer and later went to church. In the evening, she found a bible and sat on the couch reading the scriptures aloud. Radiating peace, she sat clothed, wearing none of her jewelry. The women were flabbergasted, including the staff. God's power to deliver from evil spirits is very real, as stated in Luke 10:19, "Behold, I given you authority to trample on serpents and scorpions, and over all the power of the enemy, and nothing shall by any means hurt you."

Informally, she shared her horrific story with me. She, along with seven other children, were adopted. Her adopted parents were deeply involved in witchcraft. Not only that, the father was grossly abusive. "Tick tock, nine o'clock and here he comes. My dad would punish all of us, even the boys, through sodomy," she sadly stated. How horrible, I thought. They even made her an occult prostitute at age 14, resulting in a pregnancy and uterine cancer. But now, she had Jesus.

Jesus gave His followers the power to preach, teach, heal and deliver; that authority has never been rescinded.

One day, she came frantically knocking on the door of my room. "She knows, how did she find out? I never said anything!" she began sobbing.

"Who knows what?" I answered. Her mom had discovered through divination of her conversion to Christianity and began to send fear tactics to her. I knew Jesus would help her and so we prayed. God sent another saint that was familiar with her situation. She purchased bus tickets for the young girl to San Antonio, where she would join a well-known ministry that dealt with the occult and prevailed in Jesus' name. I was so thankful. Later, she called to inform me that her parents were arrested and the father sentenced to life in prison. He was charged with rape and murder; he killed the oldest son for trying to stop the sexual abuse. Thankfully, the remaining children are now safe.

We continued the bible studies until our stay there had ended. God was touching the women and changing them, in the midst of this instable environment. We stayed at this shelter for forty-five days. Up until now, the Lord had provided for our physical needs through the shelters and granted me veteran's education benefits for school; yet, we were still displaced and unsure of where to settle. In this moment of uncertainty, an offer was presented via email from Nigeria. Some bankers discovered one of their clients had died and left millions of dollars dormant in his account. They did not know much of the deceased family, only that he was an American. This email was an offer to become the beneficiary, allowing rights to inherit the money. At first, I thought that perhaps this was a miracle, so I naively agreed to the offer.

They wanted me to sign documents and send them my bank information. Well, this made me skeptical, so I requested more information from them. They sent pictures of family, passports, and legal documents declaring me as the beneficiary. This was enough proof for me, but unfortunately, this was not the Lord's will. He showed me through a daytime vision a picture of a noose. I asked the Lord what it meant. He told me that if I went through with this deal, I would die. Whether this death was physical or spiritual, I took heed. Immediately, I emailed them back to cancel the agreement.

It later turned out that these people were trying to legally embezzle funds. To carry out the scheme, they needed someone in America to legitimize the transaction. The banker returned my email, stating that, if I did not continue with the transaction, he was going to kill himself. I never returned their emails, and cancelled my bank and email accounts. I was so thankful to God for warning me. He later gave me assurance that He had erased my handwriting and I was free from this shady and potentially dangerous transaction. For the scriptures says in Mark 8:36, "For what will it profit a man if gains the whole world and loses his soul?"

The end of our stay was approaching and I prayed for guidance for where the Lord wanted us to go. He said we were going to the coast. We then got another referral to another shelter. We traveled from the extreme north side of the city to the extreme south. This time, we were led straight to the facility. It was a huge brick house, at least three or four thousand square feet, located at the end of a street near a nursing home. The city was called Webster, located only a few miles away from the NASA Space Center.

The shelter house was packed. I heard the intake workers declining women and referring them to other shelters. We were blessed to get in. We met the women and I wanted to start the bible study there, once we got settled in. I was able to continue my education and enroll the children in school. The landscape was beautiful; the shopping centers were clean and expansive and the sky was astoundingly clear. We got settled and they allowed us to stay there for up to a year. This was sufficient time for us to make preparations to find a more permanent place to live.

One of the ladies invited us to her church. She had only one child, a six-year-old boy. He suffered from a terrible outbreak of warts that plagued his hands and toes. The condition was so severe, the other children teased him relentlessly and he wanted to kill himself. His mother tried to get them frozen off, but it didn't work. The doctors prescribed every medicine relating to the condition, but the warts returned.

The night before they left, the Lord prompted me to pray for him and anoint his infection with anointing oil. In Ephesians 5:14, it states that elders of the church should pray for the sick, anointing them with oil. At six, the young boy had accepted Jesus in his heart. With permission, he allowed me to anoint his hands and feet and pray for his healing. It was about a month later when I would hear from them again. They invited us over to see their new place. Her son came down the stairs, modeling his baby soft hands. "Hey, look at you! You're healed!" I exclaimed. He just blushed. His mother said the night they left, two of the biggest ones fell off. In about another couple of weeks, there were all gone for good. Praise the Lord! I was overjoyed for them. This was only the beginning of the miracles that Jesus would perform.

We were granted permission to have a bible study at this shelter. Some gave their life to Jesus and others were healed emotionally. I will never forget this one particular resident. She told me privately that she was stricken with Hepatitis B, cancer of the uterus, bronchitis, and, on top of that, she was HIV positive. On the sides of her neck were two hard knots. It looked as if she had swallowed marbles. Recently, she gave her life to Christ, but thought it was too late. "Maybe God is punishing me," she sighed. I reassured her that God was not mad at her and that He wanted her healed. In tears, we prayed the prayer of faith concerning her healing.

The next morning, she rushed over to me, placing my hands over her neck where the knots used to be. They were gone. "Oh, my! God does care!" she exclaimed. About a couple of weeks later, she retook the HIV test. The doctors were expecting her call. They told her that her result came back negative; the odds of that happening were .00002 percent. They gave her a copy of the negative report, which she graciously shared with me. She joyfully proclaimed the news of her healing to the others. The staff wasn't convinced, but she and I both knew that God had healed her of HIV!

Compared to the tragic experiences suffered by some of the other residents, my situation seemed like a petty quarrel. One woman shared her story of mental and sexual abuse. Her husband discovered she was leaving. "This is my gift from me to you." He infected her with the Herpes Simplex virus. Others came in with swollen eyes and busted lips. One family had an eleven–year-old daughter who was molested and gave birth to a child. These shelter ministries are truly a blessing. They try their best to help the women move on with their lives while providing support during the recovery process. I was thankful to be there. The Lord knew what we needed and who needed us.

During our stay at this shelter, the Lord revealed the ministry He wanted me to start—a children's ministry. He gave me the name and then confirmed it through someone else. Okay, I'm supposed to be working with children, but how and when? My degree was in Art. Step by step, I trusted the Lord to guide me. The shelter paid for my summer tuition and this allowed me to transfer to the University of Houston. With God, all things are possible. We stayed at this shelter for about eight months and we were ready to move on. They referred us to a transitional housing program in Galveston. These were fully furnished, two story duplexes that used to be officer barracks for the military. We had our own little townhouse, located across from the beachfront. It was like a vacation home and we definitely needed to relax.

"And these signs shall follow those who believe; In my name they shall cast out demons… they shall lay hands on the sick and they will recover."
Mark 16:17-18

Beyond The Visible

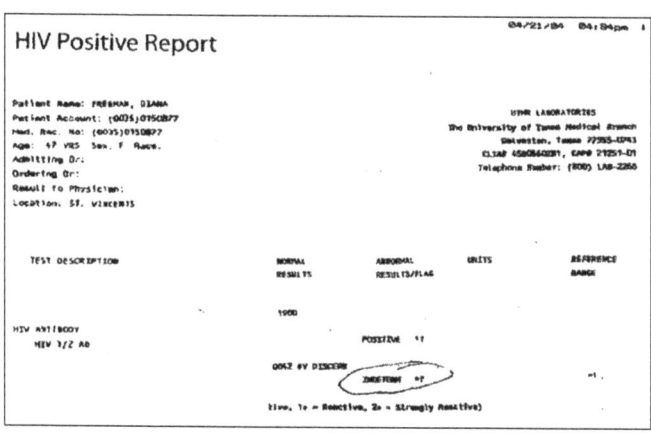

5

Divine Protection

The transitional housing program allowed us to stay there for two years. We desperately needed a new church to call home. A friend in one of my classes referred us to a nondenominational church that was about twenty minutes up the road. When we visited this church, it felt like we had found what we were looking for. It was a mixed congregation with prosperous looking people that worshiped and praised the Lord with enthusiasm. I was so excited about this church. Assuming my new role as chauffeur, we transported our neighbors without vehicles to church. I asked the Lord if He would bless me with a van so that I could take more people. Within a month, I had a van. The Lord had given me favor with the car dealer who sold my husband and I vehicles. It was at this church that the Lord clarified my purpose and specific assignment through prophesies.

During a three-day conference, which they called a "camp meeting," something incredible happened. Some of the most spiritually-gifted and well-known ministers were guest speakers. After the first night of the camp meeting, the Lord's power struck the children's ministry. When I entered the children's facility, I noticed my oldest son was laid out on the altar, trembling and crying with his hands elevated. I didn't know what to think. "Are you his mother?" the minister asked as he beckoned me to approach the altar. They anointed our foreheads with oil, explaining that we were set apart for a specific work for the Lord.

The laying of hands is an act of spiritual impartation and commissioning.

The minister and his wife were visiting children missionaries. They traveled the country teaching and raising children evangelists. Three months later, I was working in the children's ministry at this church. God had given me a program inspiration for the 4-year-olds. The church granted me the freedom to implement ideas and provided the support I needed. I really enjoyed teaching the children and watching them grow in the Lord. Little did I know, the Lord had another assignment in mind, one that I was not expecting.

Meanwhile, our cozy townhome community turned into a haven for unwanted guests. My children were afraid to be alone left alone anywhere in the house. They attested to seeing images move on the wall murals and hearing strange noises. Before we moved in, I anointed the house with oil and blessed it. I thought that was sufficient for clearing out any evil spirits that may be lingering around. To my surprise, the other women were experiencing unusual events in their homes, as well. One neighbor reported actually seeing a little boy closing one of the bedroom doors. I don't believe in ghosts, but I do believe what the bible says in Ephesians 6:12 "for we wrestle not against flesh and blood, but against principalities, against powers, against rulers of darkness of this age, against spiritual hosts of wickedness in the heavenly places." Furthermore, in Matthew 12:43, it states "When the unclean spirit is gone out of man, he goes through dry places, seeking rest and finds none."

Perhaps these evil spirits were returning to a familiar location. Nevertheless, they were trespassing. One day, I prayed and asked the Lord to reveal any evil spirits in the house. He told me to check the fireplace. A mural of a desert landscape sat over the fireplace. We purchased the picture from a resale shop. When I removed it from the wall, there it was, a streak of black smoke stained in the paint. This was not there before. We disposed of the picture and washed the wall with bleach. And in the name of Jesus, we commanded the portal shut.

A month later, around two or three a.m., I heard a baby splashing in the bathtub. My eyes were closed and I just listened. The bathroom door opened and I heard footsteps enter my bedroom. Immediately, I opened my eyes, but no one was there. Within the same timeframe, we purchased a used computer that had game software already installed. My youngest son wanted to play the game, so we opened it. To our dismay, a fortune teller appeared on the screen, reading a crystal ball.

My son, mesmerized by the image, was thrown off the bed into a violent rage. When I attempted to reboot, the computer froze, locking the image on the screen. In the name of Jesus, we commanded the evil spirit to leave. Immediately, soundness returned to my son's spirit as he sat on the bed in my arms. The Lord had already revealed to me how the enemy uses movies, video games and music to attack our children. I was determined not to have any of the enemy's trash in my house. We stood on our authority in the name of Jesus, and rid our home of these freeloaders.

In the midst of this, my husband hired a private detective and located us at the church. For the first time in a long time, I was scared. Over three years had elapsed without any notification of our whereabouts. Thankfully, the actions of the church's security prevented a potentially hostile confrontation. The children's director and I prayed for protection as we drove home that night. As soon as we entered the highway, he appeared in the rearview mirror.

Suddenly, thank God for the suddenly, my eldest son noticed we were entering pitch black darkness. Over the bridge, the city had had a power outage. Piercing through the darkness, the tail lights from the car ahead of us guided us across the bridge. When the opportunity arose, I swiftly made a hard, unexpected u-turn and headed north out of the city. When

I looked back, he was gone. Thank you Jesus. I was not prepared to meet my husband. The Lord was truly watching over us.

Resolution to this issue was inevitable. Unfortunately, the only peaceful avenue was to adjudicate. Divorce papers were served within days of the church visit. Although I couldn't afford a lawyer, I was confident that God would intervene on my behalf. At church, the children's director gave me a referral to a lawyer. This lawyer never confirmed whether or not she could help. The counselor at the transitional program, along with one of the shelter advocates, escorted me to the trial. My heart was racing, I didn't know what to expect.

Entering the courtroom, they sat on the left side and we migrated towards the opposite side. I glanced around, hoping to find the referral lawyer. Praying under my breath, I could sense the Lord's presence. Our case was announced, still no lawyer. As I stood to state my position, out of nowhere approached this petite, short-haired lady. She interceded and immediately informed the court that I resided in Galveston County with my children and motioned to transfer the litigation. The judge granted the petition. Thank you Jesus! Exuberant and relieved, I stood in awe of how perfectly the Lord orchestrated these events. As the old' saying goes, "He may not come when you want Him to, but He is always on time."

The counselor at the transitional housing unit urged me to file for a protective order. I agreed, hoping it would strengthen my defense in the temporary orders hearing for determining custody.

Unfortunately, this was not the Lord's will. However, I was disobedient and convinced myself to proceed, for the sake of the children.

The hearing went totally in favor of my husband and the request was denied. The District Attorney concluded that I had waited too long to file. "You do realize that six pieces of paper cannot protect you anyway," she gently advised. I was so convicted and repented of this foolish mistake. I should've trusted the Lord, after all, He had proven on numerous occasions to be my sole protector. When I prayed about it, I read 1 Corinthians 6, "If then you have judgments concerning things pertaining to this life, why do you appoint those who are least esteemed by the church to judge? I say this to your shame."

This situation resembled the story of King David in 1 Samuel 24. He was chased and treated like a criminal by a jealous King Saul; yet, David respected King Saul's position as the Lord's anointed and never put his hand against him, even when given the opportunity. Overall, I was grateful to receive the Lord's mercy.

Meanwhile, matters at the church had taken a serious turn for the worse. I began to feel targeted. The pastor invited ministers from around the country to preach at the church. The Holy Spirit began speaking through these ministers. They prophesied and confirmed the things the Lord had spoken to me, only more detailed.

During this awkward period, I attempted to be self-effacing, but the Lord wanted me to speak. When I didn't, He led one of His outspoken children to speak on my behalf. In response, I wrote letters to the pastor relaying the Lord's messages. The Lord wanted them to help the poor and cease idolizing their money and possessions. He used the letters to usher in miraculous events.

Appalled at the content of the letters, they refuted the message. In reality, the odds were truly against me. But in the supernatural realm, I could sense the angelic forces that surrounded me, because I stood up for what was right. God showed them great mercy in allowing them time to consider His will, even though they continued to disbelieve. They were too focused on the messenger rather than the message. I prayed for them to see the truth and hoped that they would seek guidance and restoration from the Lord. God did indeed move on the pastor's heart. He preached his next sermon with a change of heart and renewed humility. As a result, the Lord granted a tremendous miracle. That same week, he received national exposure from the most distinguished news broadcasting programs in the country—for absolutely free! The estimated value of this exposure was well over hundreds of thousands of dollars. Unfortunately, he constantly vacillated between the truth and a lie. Before long, he took credit for what the Lord had done at the expense of his ministry.

One day, while taking out the trash, I noticed that the electrical pole in front of the complex was on fire. The wooden pole was shaped in the image of cross. Strangely, only one side of it burned, never spreading. This odd occurrence reminded me of the two thieves that died on Calvary with Jesus—one on

His left and the other His right. The meaning of this event was uncovered. God knows the secret things in our hearts, as the scripture says in Jeremiah 17:9-10, "The heart is deceitful above all things, and desperately wicked; who can know it? I, the Lord, search the heart, I test the mind."

Prior to this event, another bizarre incident occurred. While on my way down the stairs of my house, an electric jolt pierced the socket of my right hip, causing the entire right side of my body to go numb. As I fell to the ground, my children flew to my side, totally baffled. "Pray for your mother!" I exclaimed. Earnestly, they hovered over me, praying for healing. Within a few minutes, the numbness subsided as I slowly regained control. What happened? It was another encounter with an angel who came to hinder my recklessness. Because the Lord was using me in such a powerful way, in the ministry and through miracles, I subtly became prideful. Quickly, I repented and the Lord forgave me. Just like the thief that acknowledged his sinfulness and was accepted, I too was in need of the Lord's mercy.

A few months later, a group of Mormons came by the house. I wasn't familiar with this religion because their badges read "Church of Jesus Christ of Latter-day Saints." I welcomed them in with the hopes of encouraging them in the truth of the gospel message. However, they insisted on studying their "Mormon book" and said it contained the "real" truth. I wouldn't allow them to open it in the house and politely escorted them out.

That night, a ferocious wind blew the hinges off my screen door. Ironically, it didn't affect any of my neighbors. After I prayed, the Lord revealed to me that Mormons were an occult religion. I should have never let them in the house. When they came back, I told them that their religion opposed the truth of the gospel and that salvation is through faith in Christ alone. One of them took offense and cursed me as they left.

Shortly after that, I discovered dead birds in the front yard and the children found human feces on our back door in the form of swear words. It sounded like witch craft. At this point, I couldn't assume that anyone did it. Satan was the only one to blame. But no matter what insults or hexes or curses were aimed at us, the Lord kept us safe.

After a while, my resolve began to slip. I was focusing on my personal prosperity too much. I noticed that my prayers were self-absorbed. The church environment began to affect me. One day, while driving from school, my van slowed down on the highway. It gradually pulled to side until it stopped. Right before my eyes, I saw smoke stream out from under the hood. Fire! My car was on fire! I couldn't believe it. Thankfully, the children were still at school and I wasn't too far from home. I ran as far away as I could, standing at a distance watching the flames consume from the front through the middle. I was thankful that the Lord saved me. I asked the Lord to examine my heart and forgive me for entertaining idolatry.

Without transportation, it was difficult to do anything. No one at the church offered to help with my situation. It was just me and Jesus again. My time at the housing program was ending. By the grace of God, I completed my bachelor's degree at the University of Houston in Art. Still, I wasn't prepared to do anything with it. I wanted to wait on the Lord for His guidance. In my heart, I knew the Lord had good things in store for us.

Two months before our departure, the temporary court hearing was set in Galveston. The Lord did not want me to get a lawyer, I had to trust that he would intervene again. This hearing would determine the primary custody of the children and liability for child support. I looked over at my husband who was accompanied by his lawyer and mother. They confidently sat in their seats expecting a smooth victory. The judge allowed me to speak. I prayed for the Lord to give me the words to say and he did. His lawyer approached the bench with a "hurry up let's get this over" look. When the judge granted me primary custody and ordered him to pay child support, their mouths plummeted to the floor. I eagerly wanted to shout, but managed to hold my composure until the trial ended.

Finally it was over. No more running and hiding, ducking and dodging. It was settled. Vengeance is mine declares, the Lord. This was an important lesson for me to learn. God was developing in me a trust in Him that was unshakable. Not only that, he wanted me to focus on remaining in forgivness and love, while He handled my problems.

Not soon after the hearing, my ex-husband and I came to amiable terms. We were able to relate to each other in a peaceful, respectful manner. During the entire two year period on the island, surrounded by chaos and unseen danger, the Lord kept us safe by divine protection. He allowed no one to harm us and provided for all of our needs. This is the nature of our heavenly Father.

"For You have been a shelter for me, A strong tower from the enemy."
Psalm 61:3

6

The Other Realm

The Lord reminded me of the desperate need for our children to know Him and His purpose for their lives. I viewed programs on TV urging people to give aid to foreign children dying from dirty, contaminated water. In comparison, our children in America are dying from unclean water—a polluted spiritual thirst. Many of them are turning to homosexual lifestyles, committing suicide, having children at young ages, strung out on drugs, victims of domestic violence, and the list goes on. With God's help, I was ready to take on the challenge of teaching them the bible and leading them to Jesus.

The Lord was ready to perform another miracle. He blessed me with a job that transitioned us into our new community. The children's court-ordered summer visitation with their father was ending and I had not secured a dwelling place yet, or transportation. After prayer, I found a new house for rent located minutes from the job. The landlords were generous enough to pick me up from work to show me the home. When we pulled into the subdivision, a beautiful lake with a waterfall welcomed us. The colonial style roads led to a set of amazing statuettes of children playing. This confirmed for me the Lord's will for the children's ministry.

The next morning, it was business as usual. Securing transportation was first on the agenda. I contacted the nearest reputable car dealership with the expectation of purchasing a vehicle. The floor manager answered and instructed me to fax in an application. With mangled credit and insufficient work stability, there was plenty of room for a miracle. With God all things are possible. The floor manager agreed to drive me to the dealership. That day, I drove home with a fairly new vehicle for only $300 down. Our God is truly awesome. In less than a month, the Lord blessed me with a job, a new house and a vehicle—God is awesome.

During the first week after we moved in, an awkward feeling lingered in the atmosphere. I could not comprehend it. The home was brand new and we were the first residents. Black widows had nested in the garage and we found other "little tenants" in the house—fire ants. They were everywhere. Lord, I just wanted to rest. In addition, the "tormentors" start calling. These were bill collectors from past debts I acquired while married. They harangued me for payments and threatened lawsuits. The presence of evil was so strong; it was like Satan himself was hovering around me.

Beyond The Visible

Physically, there was no place to rest and I fell into a dark, deep unexplainable depression. My whole countenance sank. I decided I wasn't going to sleep; all I wanted to do was have a pity party. My mother called and interrupted the fiesta. The Holy Spirit revealed to her that something was wrong with her daughter. "I don't know what's up with you, but you need to go to bed! Go straight to bed! You are strong in the Lord and God has your back," she insisted. My mother had given her life to Christ and encouraged me on many occasions.

After quoting a few scriptures and rebuking the devil, my faith strengthened. The next task on the "to do" list was to find a new church. A friend had suggested this non-denominational church in the area, so we went there. The worship was awesome, you could feel the presence of God; however, I noticed it was a rather small congregation for the size of the building. I thought perhaps they had just moved in, but I was mistaken. Once again, the gift of prophecy was powerful at this church. Unfortunately, they did not welcome or accept us. Even though we said nothing, the negative energy spoke loud and clear. Emotionally, I was drained from the disappointing church experiences.

At about 2 or 3 a.m. one night, I couldn't sleep again. My heart ached after witnessing the divisiveness amongst the Lord's people. On my knees, I cried out to the Lord for comfort and strength. Before the prayer was over, I found myself worshiping God on my face. As I lifted my head above the floor, place directly in front of me was a craft my son had colored earlier. It was a badge that read "Brave Soldier." The lesson was the story of Joshua and how he led God's people into their promised land. Strangely, no one else was awake and the floor was clear before I began praying. An angel placed that craft, so gently and precisely, in front of me. It was just what I needed to press on.

The next Sunday, we decided to visit a church we often attended with my ex-husband. I considered it our place of refuge during transition. The people were always so warm and friendly and the leadership was trustworthy. On the second visit, I prayed and asked the Lord if we should join. For me, that meant active involvement, submission to authority, and loyalty. The answer came supernaturally.

After the church service, we got into car. My son noticed a note on the passenger seat. "How did that get in here?" I wondered. The car doors were locked and windows rolled up. The note was a printed email message. Its text read, "What took you so long to get here? Just kidding. If you need anything, just let me know." Amazing! Another angelic message of confirmation. We joined the church with the intention of sticking with our commitment and walking in love, no matter what.

By this time, I was working the full time job. It wasn't quite enough to meet our living expenses, but it was better than nothing. My boss was a Jewish man from New York and his wife owned a travel agency located in the same office. They furnished me with my own office and an enormous pile of administrative work. I felt like a Hebrew slave. The phones never stopped ringing. Exhausted from the stressful work load, I came home irritated, angry and frustrated most of the time. Not good when you have children depending on you for everything. One morning, I had an encounter that changed my life and view of finances forever.

Overly fatigued, I stretched myself on the floor and crashed with my face sunk into my bible. Lying there, a stream of cacophonies filled my ears as if I were passing through another dimension. Suddenly, two voices appeared in the room. The smurf-like voices laughed hysterically. One of them said with a caustic giggle, "Look at how exhausted they are. Let's attack them again." Immediately, I opened my eyes and only to find myself alone. I knew these were demons.

Later that day, the menacing tormentors called again. I was suddenly burdened with payments that were not anticipated that week. The Lord allowed me to encounter this experience to stir me to action. I didn't realize the enemy was trespassing by granting himself squatters-rights over my financing. As a faithful tither and giver, my blessings should never have been stolen.

The one thing I wasn't doing consistently was standing on the authority the Lord gave me as his child concerning my finances. With every attack, I had to believe I was healed and command the enemy to return sevenfold what he stole. In addition, I began to profess every scripture I knew on God's promises concerning wealth. In Deuteronomy 8:18 it states, "And He has given us the power to create to wealth."

That word power can be translated as ideas. Also, it says in Proverbs 10:22 "The blessings of the Lord makes a person rich and he adds no sorrow to it." In addition, the Lord admonished me to speak to the mountain of lack and command it to be moved. Almost immediately, I saw results. The phones calls ceased, I got an increase in my salary and the Lord granted me an income producing idea. The biblical laws of sowing and reaping are eternal and priceless. Satan will never rob me again.

Wisdom and revelation are not to be interpreted as mystical. Wisdom concerns practical, workable principles; revelation refers to clear perception and applicable understanding. The Holy Spirit is the divine and supernatural source of both.

"And my God shall supply all your need according to His riches in glory by Christ Jesus."
Philippians 4:19

7

Believing without Seeing

After six months of working on the job, the Lord told me to quit and start the children's ministry. Besides, I was tired of being away from my own children and leaving them in the hands of people whose convictions were contrary to mine.

I dreaded having to tell the boss of my resignation. He had a very quick temper and I didn't want to hear his mouth. Not my will, the Lord's will be done. January 15th was duty deadline. However, I wasn't financially prepared to make this move. As a single parent with three children, it appeared practically absurd. But I've learned to obey the Lord quickly; He always knows what is best. My faith was surely on trial. Within a month after I resigned, the Lord blessed me with over several thousand dollars from IRS refunds and back child support. Walking on the water wasn't as bad as I thought.

I received a phone call from one of the ladies that resided in the transitional housing program in Galveston. Her close friend desperately needed help. This woman had traveled from Chicago to Houston with hopes of finding a better future. She suffered years of emotional abuse from family members and severe anxiety attacks, and now she needed a place to stay because her current arrangements were not healthy. By this time, I was at home, planning and organizing the children's ministry. We had plenty of room in our two-story home, so I didn't hesitate to offer help.

After speaking with her on the phone, my initial impression was that this nice, faith-filled Christian woman just needed some encouragement and guidance. When I picked her up, I was surprised. I thought to see a homely individual, but she was dressed very elegantly. Her black leather knee-high boots and matching jacket made me think she was financially stable. Unfortunately, she was not. In addition, she was accompanied by one of her three children. Somehow, we managed to pack all eight of her overstuffed bags into my petite compact car. The car ride home was long and stuffy, but I used it to gain as much information as I could on our new friend. I sensed her nervousness and didn't want her to feel uncomfortable.

After settling in, she lit up a cigarette and began to tell her family history and how she watched our church on TV, dreaming of someday being in the sanctuary. She also informed me that she had the gift of dreams. God showed her events through her dreams and they came to pass, whether they were for her or someone else. I informed her that the gifts God gives us are for others, to help advance the kingdom of God. Perhaps the Lord had sent her here to develop those gifts in the ministry. But first, we both agreed that she needed some deliverance.

The first night, she curled up on the floor shivering and crying. Confounded, I immediately attempted an exorcism. To my surprise, she thought I was a demon. While lying on the floor, with cell phone plastered to her face, she screamed repeatedly, "It's a setup! The devil is trying to kill me!" Immediately, I began to pray and read the scriptures aloud. When she finally calmed down, she insisted that I take her to the hospital. Even though I didn't think a hospital visit was necessary, the Lord said that she needed to feel His love through me. She wanted to go to the hospital, so we went. I kept my arms around her shoulders and assured her of the Father's love for her.

Later, I learned that she found a sense of comfort in the medication the doctors prescribed for her anxiety. My first inclination was that she must have practiced divination or witchcraft. In addition, she smoked two packs of cigarettes a day. Yet her gift of dreams was amazing. During her stay with us, the Lord had shown her revelations through dreams and prophetic insights concerning my family. After praying about it, I learned that she had a calling in life and that the Lord was speaking through her. This was hard for me to swallow, considering her addictions and illness. Could God use someone in her spiritual condition? Yes, he can. Besides, he used me in my variety of predicaments. Putting aside the critical attitude, I needed to be open to what the Lord was doing in this situation.

Deep inside, she wanted to be delivered so that she could serve the Lord. She displayed tremendous faith in uprooting from her familiar surroundings of thirty years to relocate to an unknown place. I repented for my degrading and prideful attitude towards her.

We went to church and she was overwhelmed. Her faith skyrocketed after listening to the message. The next morning, she heard the Lord tell her to go and see the house that she dreamt of. That afternoon, we went out driving to find it. On the side of the highway, a sign read "Zero Money Down Move In." "That sounds like it's for me," she exclaimed. After prayer, we went to the new home site, not knowing what to expect. It was love at first sight. With camera in hand, we took pictures of her in the model home of her choice. As we toured the neighborhood, she nearly jumped out the car when saw the home she dreamt of. There wasn't a sold sign, so we assumed it was available.

Faith is established conviction concerning things unseen and settled expectation of future reward.

Immediately, we returned to the salesman to inquire about the house. The address was "7707." Seven, the number meaning perfection in Christ, evidenced our faith that this was the house. Ironically, the salesman couldn't find the home on the map or the address. By this time, our faith adrenaline propelled. While the salesman researched the home, she wondered if it had a contract pending. "If there is one, they will cancel it," I told her.

We met the salesman at the house only to hear that there *was* a contract on the house. He wanted to show us other homes that were available, but I knew that that was her house. Right as we were heading out of the area, he got a phone call that the contract had canceled. Halleluiah! The Lord was moving on our behalf, honoring our faith, as it states in Hebrews 11:6, "It is impossible to please God without faith." He showed us the inside of the house and it was beautiful. The next question arose about financing. She looked at me and I looked back at her. We told him that we would get back with him. I could sense her faith beginning to falter. She had only been in Texas for a month and her employment history was unstable. Despite the dilemma, the Lord had blessed her with a gift for floral. I encouraged her to pray and seek the Lord for wisdom. Perhaps, God could bless her gift with flowers as an income producing avenue. Convinced, she began designing arrangements for products.

Her faith soon dwindled as she became overwhelmed by the task. From that moment, things went in the opposite direction. She started doubting God and speaking negatively. The cell phone became the hell phone as she would speak death to her friends and family about her situation. Truthfully, my patience was running thin. I did my best to help and had to trust God to take care of her. Prayer helped me stay focused. Unfortunately, her son became homesick and she spoke of leaving. Now her faith turned into to fear, which produced the end result; a trip back to Chicago.

I learned much from that situation and all of the divine encounters that I have been privileged to experience. The Lord's mercy is truly remarkable and we cannot judge people based on appearance. People are in desperate need to see the love of God though the lives of his people. Most importantly, faith in God is crucial to the Christian walk. It is not prejudiced, confined, or limited to the salvation experience. Faith was the very thing that God used to guide, protect and deliver me. It is what distinguishes the true Christians from the pretenders. For scripture says, in Habakkuk 2:4 "The just shall live by his faith." In addition, miracles can and will happen if you believe.

We are expecting God to do beyond what we could ever ask, think or imagine in regards to reaching this younger generation with the gospel of Jesus Christ. Even now, the Lord has tremendously blessed our minute efforts to launch the children's ministry in our community. We have the awesome privilege of raising a chosen generation, a royal priesthood of radical little soldiers for Jesus. The best is yet to come.

As a child of God, I am no longer victim to my circumstances or anything the devil would try to throw at me. More than a conqueror, standing in the strength and power of Almighty God is my position. My desire is for everyone to have an intimate relationship with Jesus. That's His desire also. He cares about what we care about. Not only that, He wants to show us His power, love and trust. The awesome thing about God is that He knows all of our shortcomings, failures, and backgrounds and yet He still loves us. His workmanship in our lives is able to weave everything we've experienced, both the good and bad, into His wonderful master plan.

If you have read this book and think, "well that was an interesting story," let me encourage you in this. The Lord has a plan and purpose for your life too. The key to discovering it is a personal relationship with Jesus. A simple prayer is all that's needed. Right now, He's listening. Say, Lord Jesus, I repent of my sins. I believe you are God's son and you died for me. Come into life and be my Lord and Savior. If you prayed that prayer sincerely, get ready for a remarkable adventure!

"Go into the world and preach the gospel to every creature."
Mark 16:15

Lightning Source UK Ltd.
Milton Keynes UK
UKHW011046091221
395376UK00002B/313